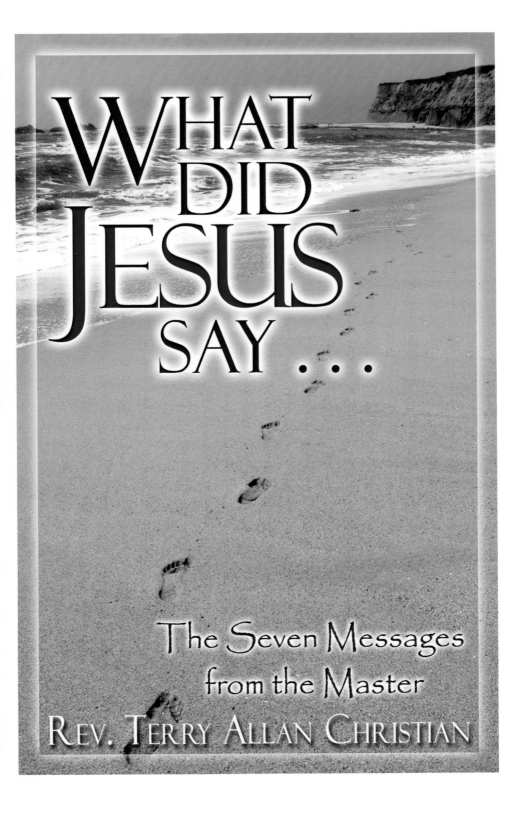

WHAT DID JESUS SAY ...

The Seven Messages from the Master

REV. TERRY ALLAN CHRISTIAN

WHAT DID JESUS SAY...

The Seven Messages from the Master

Graphic Design & Page Layout
Right By Design Media Solutions

www.DivinePublications.info

Divine Publications

WHAT DID JESUS SAY...

A Special Gift

for

From

Date

This book is dedicated
to everyone who wants to:
walk with Jesus, feel His presence,
hear His words, and understand
His Teachings.

PREFACE

A Personal Note to the Reader

The book you are holding is a one of a kind book. It wasn't written by me, it was composed by me, with the guidance of The Holy Spirit.

Ten years ago I was led to gather and organize the Teachings of Jesus into a special book, using only the words spoken by Him and nothing more. Taking the red-letter edition of the New King James Bible, I began the task of setting apart the words in red. In my obedience to the Lord, and by the grace of God **.....** *I now give you this book!*

The Seven Messages from the Master have been carefully organized to clearly reveal the Teachings of Jesus without the distractions of the religious and political conflicts of His time. You will quickly notice that the scriptures are taken out of order and composed together in this book. The intent of this book is to put you, the reader, into an imagined walk along the beach with Jesus. I've made note at the bottom of each page where the exact location, chapter and verse can be found in your Bible... for your additional study.

After you've completed your walk with Jesus, you will have read over 500 Bible passages spoken directly by Him. And when you're done, I encourage you to dig deeper into the Gospels in order to more fully grasp God's Word and Will for your life.

Truly, I wish for you a most peaceful walk with Jesus, and I look forward to meeting you one day in the future, when all of us become One Flock, together, with One Shepherd.

In HIS LOVE I serve

Rev. Terry Allan Christian
January 2012

If anyone loves Me,
he will keep My word;

and My Father will love him,

and We will come to him
and make Our home with him.

He who does not love Me
does not keep My words;

and the word which you hear
is not Mine but the Father's
who sent Me.

-Jesus Christ

WHAT DID JESUS SAY...

The Seven Messages from the Master

Table of Contents

Introduction
The Seven Messages from the Master

Imagine you're walking down the beach. You come across a crowd of Believers, waiting for Jesus to appear and teach them. What would He say? Would He spend time talking about religious and political conflicts? Or would He speak about Love, Light and Truth?

Join us, as we go for a walk with Jesus, and listen to His words. Listen as He shares with us, the Seven Messages from the Master. Each spiritual message reveals His teachings that will strengthen you and guide you to a most peaceful life in Christ.

The First Message is **The Christ**. This message contains the declaration from Jesus that He is The Christ. The **One** who has come down from Heaven. Not to do His own will but to do the will of God the Father, who sent Him. It is because of Jesus the Christ that we are called the *Children of God*. What an honor it is for each of us to be invited into the heavenly realm - the spiritual world within where we can live as "One with God". The name "*Christian*" comes from being a "follower of Christ." It was Jesus who said, "I have given you an example that you should do as I have done to you."

The Second Message is **The Father and The Son**. In this message Jesus tells us about His loving relationship with our Heavenly Father. It's here that Jesus demonstrates His respect, obedience and willingness to do whatever His Father in Heaven tells Him. Jesus celebrates His relationship with His Heavenly Father and invites us to do like-wise with Him.

Jesus instructs us to "be perfect as (our) Father in heaven is perfect."

As you read this message, think about this question...
         If God is your Father, what kind of child are you?

The Third Message is **The Word**. In this message, Jesus teaches us about The Word. The first chapter of the Gospel of John says, "...the Word became flesh and dwelt among us, and we beheld His glory." (John 1:14)

Jesus said, "By your words, you will be justified, and by your words, you will be condemned."

The Fourth Message is **I AM the Way, the Truth and the Life**. In this message, Jesus teaches us how to live a Spiritual Life. All the lessons that we need to learn to live in peace and harmony - without fear and judgment - are in this message. This message will calm the mind and heal the heart. It will restore and revitalize the life of anyone who is willing to be a true disciple of Christ.

Whatever your situation - whatever your adversity - there IS an answer in His teachings. Now you will know for yourself, without prejudice - *What Did Jesus Say* about... love, light, truth, believing, forgiveness, prayer, faith, marriage, children, divorce, giving, charity, healing, loyalty, brotherhood, mercy, discipleship and much more.

The Fifth Message is **The Kingdom of Heaven**. In this message Jesus reveals to us a Kingdom, a heavenly place where we can have eternal life if we live our life doing the will of God. One of the most important statements in this message, is when Jesus said, "Not everyone who says to me, 'Lord, Lord' shall enter The Kingdom of Heaven, but He who does the will of My Father in Heaven." This means that the "Kingdom of Heaven" is a "place" we are allowed to enter, and the key to the gate is in doing the will of The Father in Heaven. Jesus said, "...unless we are converted and become as little children, we will by no means enter the Kingdom of Heaven."

The Sixth Message is **The End Times**. With all of the political turmoil and social tensions surrounding us in the world today, it doesn't take much to imagine a world conflict on a biblical level. The events of 9/11 have taught us how quickly our lives can change. The world we live in is very tense. This tension demonstrates itself everyday by the violence of one man to another; one country against another, and finally, religions attacking other religions - all in the name of their 'god'. Jesus said, "take heed and beware... and pray that you may be counted worthy to escape all these things that will come to pass. He who endures to the end shall be saved."

The Seventh Message is **The Holy Spirit**. In this message Jesus reveals the inner-voice that guides us to "all truth" including the truth in these Spiritual Messages. Jesus said that the Holy Spirit is sent here on purpose to convict the world of sin, and to be a comforter, a helper, and a teacher for each of us. The Holy Spirit is that still small voice within every Christian believer. Wherever we go, He is there waiting for us - because He is in us. We have all felt the presence of this loving spirit. Jesus said, "the Holy Spirit will guide you into all truth."

Finally, the walk ends when Jesus says His Last Prayer. In this prayer, Jesus prays to His Father for His Disciples and for all those who believe in His words. He doesn't pray for the world, He prays for those who believe in Him.

Jesus said, "You believe in God, believe also in Me."

My promise to you: Every time you walk with Jesus, and meditate on His Spiritual Messages, you will discover a renewed strength and discipline in your Christian walk. And, you'll develop a personal closer relationship with Jesus Christ at the same time.

I pray that *The Seven Messages from the Master,* will help you find a greater way to serve and worship our Heavenly Father. And may each day with the Lord lift you high enough to see YOUR Heavenly Place.

-Reverend Christian

Walking with the Master

One night a man had a dream, he was walking along the beach with the LORD.

Across the sky flashed scenes from his life,
and for each scene he noticed
two sets of footprints:
one belonging to him,
and the other to the LORD.

As his life flashed before him,
he noticed that many times during his life
there was only one set of footprints.

He also noticed that it happened
at the lowest and saddest
times in his life. This bothered him,
so he questioned the LORD, asking,

"I don't understand why,
when I needed you most,
you would leave me?"

and the LORD replied:
"My precious child, I love you and I would never leave you.
During your times of trial and suffering, when you see only
one set of footprints, it was then that I carried you."

Footprints in the Sand by Mary Stevenson
Re-written by Rev. Terry Allan Christian

The Spiritual Messages that follow
come directly from the * words of Jesus
as they were recorded in the
New King James Bible
and then printed in red.

The page headers colored in BLUE
are meant to bridge the scriptures together.
These words were spoken by Jesus in the Bible,
though not in the context referenced on the page.

We believe each message
is a faithful representation
of the Love, Light and Truth
of His Teachings.

* scripture reference
at the bottom of each page.

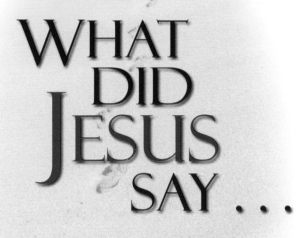

WHAT DID JESUS SAY ...

The Seven Messages from the *Master*

*In the Beginning was the Word,
and the Word was with God,
and the Word was God.*

He was in the Beginning with God.

*All things were made through Him,
and without Him nothing was made
that was made.
In Him was life, and that life was
the light of men.*

*As many as received Him, to them He gave
the right to become children of God,
to those who believe in His name;
who were born, not of blood,
nor of the will of the flesh, nor of the will of man,
but of God.*

*And the Word became flesh
and dwelt among us,
and we beheld His glory.*

John 1 : 1-4, 12-14

Follow Me,
and I will make you become fishers of men.

Mark 1:17

MESSAGE 1

The Christ

*It is early morning, and as the sun is rising over the water,
you could see that the crowd of believers were already gathering
at the waters edge, waiting for Jesus to appear,
and to teach them.
As the crowd began to calm down, a silence arose
to such a degree, that you could hear the birds flying above.*

And then Jesus appeared, and said...

Peace be with you my brothers and sisters

I AM the Christ

I have come down from heaven,
not to do My own will,
but the will of Him who sent Me.

John 6:38

Truly, I Say to You

The Spirit of the Lord
is upon Me,

because He hath anointed Me
to preach the gospel to the poor;

He hath sent Me to heal the brokenhearted,

To proclaim liberty to the captives
And recovering of sight to the blind,

And

To set at liberty those who are oppressed.

Luke 4:18

4

Therefore,
I say to you who hear,

Come to Me, all you who labor
and are heavy laden,
and I will give you rest.

Take My yoke upon you
and learn from Me,
for I am gentle and lowly in heart,
and you will find rest for your souls.

For My yoke is easy
and my burden is light.

Matthew 11:28-30

5 *The Christ*

If anyone desires to come after Me,

let him deny himself,
and take up his cross daily, and follow Me.

For whoever desires to save his life will
lose it, but whoever loses his life
for My sake will find it.

For what profit is it to a man
if he gains the whole world,
and loses his own soul?

Or what will a man give
in exchange for his soul?

Matthew 16:24-26

Again I Say

If anyone thirsts,
let him come to Me and drink.

He who believes in Me, as the Scripture has said,
out of his heart will flow rivers of living water.

And

If anyone serves Me, let him follow Me; and
where I am, there My servant will be also. If
anyone serves Me, him My Father will honor.

John 7:37-38 / John 12:26

The Christ

Now take heed and listen

*Do not think that I came
to bring peace on earth.
I did not come to bring peace
but a sword.*

*For I have come to
set a man against his father,
a daughter against her mother,
and a daughter-in-law
against her mother-in-law*

*and a man's enemies will be those
of his own household.*

Matthew 10:34-36

Therefore

He who loves father or mother
more than Me is not worthy of Me.

And he who loves son or daughter
more than Me is not worthy of Me.

And he who does not take his cross and
follow after Me is not worthy of Me.

And
I say to you who hear,

He who finds his life will lose it,
and he who loses his life for My sake will find it.

Matthew 10:37-39

The Christ

Most assuredly, I say to you,
he who does not enter the sheepfold by the door,
but climbs up some other way,
the same is a thief and a robber.

But he who enters by the door
is the shepherd of the sheep.
To him the doorkeeper opens,
and the sheep hear his voice;
and he calls his own sheep by name
and leads them out.

And when he brings out his own sheep,
he goes before them; and the sheep follow him,
for they know his voice.
Yet they will by no means follow a stranger,
but will flee from him,
for they do not know the voice of strangers."

John 10:1-5

Most assuredly, I say to you, I am the door of
the sheep. All who ever came before Me are thieves
and robbers, but the sheep did not hear them.

I am the door.
If anyone enters by Me, he will be saved,
and will go in and out and find pasture.

The thief does not come except to steal,
and to kill, and to destroy.
I have come that they may have life,
and that they may have it more abundantly.

I am the good shepherd.
The good shepherd gives His life for the sheep.

But a hireling, he who is not the shepherd,
one who does not own the sheep, sees the wolf
coming and leaves the sheep and flees;
and the wolf catches the sheep and scatters them.
The hireling flees because he is a hireling
and does not care about the sheep.

John 10:7-13

The Christ

I am the good shepherd; and I know My sheep,
and am known by My own.

And

As the Father knows Me,
even so I know the Father and I lay
down my life for the sheep.

And other sheep I have which are not of this fold;
them also I must bring and they will hear My voice:

and there will be one flock and one shepherd.

John 10:14-16

12

Listen Closely

My sheep hear My voice,
and I know them, and they follow Me.

And I give them eternal life,
and they shall never perish;
neither shall anyone snatch them
out of My hand.

My Father, who has given them to Me,
is greater than all;
and no one is able to snatch them
out of My Father's hand.

Truly
I say to you who hear,

"I and My Father are One."

John 10:27-30

The Christ

Now,
let these Words sink down in your ears.

I am the true vine,
and My Father is the vinedresser.

Every branch in Me
that does not bear fruit He takes away;
and every branch that bears fruit
He prunes, that it may bear more fruit.

Abide in Me, and I in you.

As the branch cannot bear fruit of itself,
unless it abides in the vine,
neither can you,
unless you abide in Me.

John 15:1,2,4

14

Assuredly, I Say to You

I am the vine, you are the branches.
He who abides in Me, and I in him,
bears much fruit;
for without Me you can do nothing.

If anyone does not abide in Me,
he is cast out as a branch and is withered;
and they gather them and throw them into the fire,
and they are burned.

If you abide in Me, and My words abide in you,
you will ask what you desire and
it shall be done for you.

And by this My Father is glorified,
that you bear much fruit;
so you will be My disciples.

John 15:5-8

Peace be with you.

Then Jesus started walking and they followed Him

End of Message

The Christ

MESSAGE II

The Father and The Son

The morning sun is now shining, and as more believers began to arrive, Jesus turned around and said...

Now I want to tell you about My Father

*I came forth from the Father
and have come into the world. Again,
I leave the world and go to the Father.*

John 16:28

Hear Me Everyone, and Understand

No one has ascended to heaven
but He who came down from heaven,
that is, the Son of Man who is in heaven.

And as Moses lifted up the serpent in the wilderness,
even so must the Son of Man be lifted up,
that whoever believes in Him should
not perish but have eternal life.

For God so loved the world that He gave
His only begotten Son, that whoever believes in
Him should not perish but have everlasting life.

For God did not send His Son
into the world to condemn the world,
but that the world through Him might be saved.

John 3:13-17

18

Assuredly, I Say to You

He who believes in Him is not condemned;
but he who does not believe is condemned already,
because he has not believed in the name
of the only begotten Son of God.

And this is the condemnation,
that the light has come into the world,
and men loved darkness rather than light,
because their deeds were evil.

For everyone practicing evil hates the light
and does not come to the light,
lest his deeds should be exposed.

But he who does the truth comes to the
light, that his deeds may be clearly seen,
that they have been done in God."

John 3:18-21

Therefore, I Say to You

If anyone desires to come after Me,
let him deny himself, and take up his cross daily,
and follow Me.

For whoever desires to save his life will lose it,
but whoever loses his life for My sake will save it.

For what profit is it to a man if he
gains the whole world,
and is himself destroyed or lost?

And

Whoever is ashamed of Me and My words,
of him the Son of Man will be ashamed
when He comes in His own glory, and in
His Father's, and of the holy angels.

Luke 9:23-26

And

Whoever confesses Me before men,

*him I will also confess before
My Father who is in heaven.*

But whoever denies Me before men,

*him I will also deny before My Father
who is in heaven.*

Matthew 10:32-33

Assuredly, I Say to You,

*My Father loves Me, because I lay down
My life that I may take it again.*

*No one takes it from Me, but I lay it down
of Myself. I have power to lay it down,
and I have power to take it again. This
command I have received from My Father.*

*He who has My commandments
and keeps them, it is he who loves Me.*

*And he who loves Me will be loved by My Father,
and I will love him and manifest Myself to him.*

John 10:17-18 / 14:21

Now Listen Closely

As the Father loved Me,
I also have loved you; abide in My love.

If you keep My commandments,
you will abide in My love, just as I have
kept My Father's commandments
and abide in His love.

These things I have spoken to you,
that My joy may remain in you,
and that your joy may be full.
And,
This is my commandment
that you love one another as I have loved you.
Greater love has no one than this,
than to lay down one's life for his friends.
You are My friends if you do
whatever I command you.

John 15:9-14

I Tell You Truly,

I am the Bread which came down from heaven.

I am the bread of life.

*I am the Living Bread which came down from heaven.
if anyone eats of this bread, he will live forever.*

And

*As the living Father sent Me,
and I live because of the Father,
so he who feeds on Me
will live because of Me.*

John 6:41, 48, 51, 57

Again I say,

*All things
have been delivered to Me by
My Father, and no one knows the Son
except the Father.*

*Nor does anyone know the Father
except the Son, and the one to whom
the Son wills to reveal Him.*

*And, no one can come to Me
unless the Father who sent Me draws him;
and I will raise him up at the last day.*

Matthew 11:27 / John 6:44

The Father and The Son

Most assuredly, I say to you,

the Son can do nothing of Himself,
but what He sees the Father do;
for whatever He does,
the Son also does in like manner.

For the Father loves the Son,
and shows Him all things
that He Himself does;
and He will show Him greater works
than these, that you may marvel.

For as the Father raises the dead
and gives life to them,
even so the Son gives life to
whom He will.

John 5:19-21

The Father judges no one,
but has committed all judgment to the Son,
that all should honor the Son
just as they honor the Father.

Moreover

He who does not honor the Son
does not honor the Father
who sent Him.

John 5:22-23

Now Learn This,

I am the Way,
the Truth, and the Life.

No one comes to the Father
except through me.

I am the resurrection
and the life.

He who believes in Me,
though he may die, he shall live.

And whoever lives and believes in Me
shall never die.

John 14:6 / John 11:25-26

Most assuredly, I say to you

he who believes in Me,
the works that I do he will do also;

and greater works than these he will do,
because I go to My Father.

And

Whatever you ask in My name, that I will do,
that the Father may be glorified in the Son.

If you ask anything in My name,

I will do it.

John 14:12-14

Assuredly, I Say to You

All that the Father gives Me will come to Me,
and the one who comes to Me
I will by no means cast out.

For I have come down from heaven,
not to do My own will, but the will
of Him who sent Me.

And

This is the will of the Father who sent Me,
that of all He has given Me
I should lose nothing,
but should raise it up at the last day.

And this is the will of Him who sent Me,
that everyone who sees the Son
and believes in Him may have everlasting life;
and I will raise him up at the last day.

John 6:37-40

Again I Say

No one can come to Me unless the Father
who sent Me draws him;
and I will raise him up at the last day.

It is written in the prophets,
And they shall all be taught by God.

Therefore everyone who has heard
and learned from the Father comes to Me.

Not that anyone has seen the Father,
except He who is from God;
He has seen the Father.

Most assuredly, I say to you, he who
believes in Me has everlasting life.

John 6:44-47

31   *The Father and The Son*

Now Listen Closely

The Father has life in Himself,
so He has granted the Son to have life in
Himself, and has given Him authority to execute
judgment also, because He is the Son of Man.

Do not marvel at this; for the hour is coming
in which all who are in the graves
will hear His voice and come forth
those who have done good,
to the resurrection of life,
and those who have done evil,
to the resurrection of condemnation.

I can of Myself do nothing.
As I hear, I judge;
and My judgment is righteous,
because I do not seek My own will
but the will of the Father who sent Me.

John 5:26-30

Watch Therefore

The hour is coming,
and now is,

when the true worshipers
will worship the Father
in spirit and truth;

for the Father
is seeking such to worship Him.

God is Spirit,
and those who worship Him
must worship in spirit and truth.

John 4:23-24

Peace be with you.

Then Jesus knelt down to pray

End of Message

MESSAGE III

The Word

It's now late morning, and as the crowd of believers began to sit together, you could see that Jesus was about to teach again. The silence could be felt, all around us, as the birds could be heard, flying above...

And then Jesus stood up and said..

Now I want to teach you about the Word

It is written, man shall not live by bread alone but by every word of God.

Luke 4:4

Hear Me Everyone, and Understand

If you abide in Me, and My words
abide in you, you will ask what you desire
and it shall be done for you.

It is the Spirit who gives life;
the flesh profits nothing. The words that
I speak to you are spirit, and they are life.

Most assuredly, I say to you,
he who hears My word and believes
in Him who sent Me has everlasting life,
and shall not come into judgment,
but has passed from death into life.
And
The words that I speak to you
I do not speak on My own authority;
but the Father who dwells in Me
does the works.

John 15:7 / John 6:63 / John 5:24 / John 14:10b

Again I Say

I have not spoken on My own authority;
but the Father who sent Me
gave Me a command,

what I should say
and what I should speak.

And I know that
His command is everlasting life.

Therefore, whatever I speak,
just as the Father has told Me,
so I speak.

John 12:49-50

I Tell You Truly

If anyone loves Me, he will keep
My word; and My Father will love him, and
We will come to him and make Our home with him.

He who does not love Me does not keep My words;
and the word which you hear is not Mine
but the Father's who sent Me.

John 14:23-24

Again I Say

He who believes in Me,
believes not in Me but in Him who sent Me.
And he who sees Me sees Him who sent Me.

I have come as a light into the world,
that whoever believes in Me
should not abide in darkness

And if anyone hears My words
and does not believe, I do not judge him;
for I did not come to judge the world
but to save the world.

He who rejects Me, and does not
receive My words, has that which judges him
the word that I have spoken
will judge him in the last day.

John 12:44-48

Now Learn This,

A good tree does not bear bad fruit,
nor does a bad tree bear good fruit.

For every tree is known by its own fruit.

For men do not gather figs from thorns,
nor do they gather grapes from a bramble bush.

A good man out of the good treasure
of his heart brings forth good;

and an evil man out of the evil treasure
of his heart brings forth evil.

For out of the abundance of the heart
his mouth speaks.

Luke 6:43-45

Therefore

Whoever comes to Me, and hears My sayings
and does them,

I will show you whom he is like:
He is like a man building a house, who dug deep
and laid the foundation on the rock.

And when the flood arose,
the stream beat vehemently against the house,
and could not shake it,
for it was founded on the rock.

But he who heard and did nothing
is like a man who built a house on the earth
without a foundation, against which
the stream beat vehemently;
and immediately it fell.
And the ruin of that house was great.

Luke 6:47-49

Now let these words sink down in your ears

Behold, a sower went out to sow.
And as he sowed,
some seed fell by the wayside;
and the birds came and devoured them.

Some fell on stony places,
where they did not have much earth;
and they immediately sprang up
because they had no depth of earth.

But when the sun was up
they were scorched,
and because they had no root
they withered away.

And some fell among thorns,
and the thorns sprang up and choked them.

But others fell on good ground
and yielded a crop: some a hundredfold,
some sixty, some thirty.

He who has ears to hear, let him hear!

Matthew 13:3-9

When anyone hears the word of the kingdom,
and does not understand it, then the wicked one comes
and snatches away what was sown in his heart.
This is he who received seed by the wayside.

But he who received the seed
on stony places, this is he who hears the word
and immediately receives it with joy;
yet he has no root in himself, but
endures only for a while.
For when tribulation or persecution arises
because of the word, immediately he stumbles.

Now he who received seed
among the thorns is he who hears the word,
and the cares of this world
and the deceitfulness of riches choke the word,
and he becomes unfruitful.

But he who received seed on the good ground
is he who hears the word and understands it,
who indeed bears fruit and produces:
some a hundredfold, some sixty, some thirty.

Matthew 13:19-23

43

I Tell You Truly

Take heed what you hear.
With the same measure you use,
it will be measured to you;
and to you who hear, more will be given.

For every idle word men may speak,
they will give account of it in the day of judgment.

For by your words you will be justified,
and by your words you will be condemned.

Therefore take heed how you hear.

For whoever has, to him more will be given;
and whoever does not have, even what he
seems to have will be taken from him.

Mark 4:24 / Matthew 12:36-37 / Luke 8:18

"Most Assuredly, I say to you,"

If you abide in My word,
you are My disciples indeed.
And you shall know the truth,
and the truth shall make you free.

Heaven and earth will pass away,
but My words will by no means pass away.

And Remember Always,

Blessed are those who hear
the word of God and keep it!

John 8:31b-32 / Matthew 24:35 / Luke 11:28

Peace be with you.

Then Jesus knelt down to pray

End of Message

The Word

MESSAGE IV

*I AM the Way
the Truth and the Life*

*It is now about the noon hour, and the crowd
of believers grew even larger as they gathered by the waters edge.
When everyone quieted down, the silence could be heard
by the sounds of the birds, flying above...*

And then Jesus stood up, and said...

Now I want to teach you about Life

Can the blind lead the blind?
Will they not both fall into a ditch?

Luke 6:39

The Teachings of Jesus

Truly, I Say to You Who Hear

Enter by the narrow gate;
for wide is the gate and broad is the way
that leads to destruction,
and there are many who go in by it.

Because narrow is the gate and difficult is the way
which leads to life, and there are few who find it.

Matthew 7:13-14

Now Listen Closely

Whoever hears these sayings of Mine,
and does them, I will liken him to a wise man
who built his house on the rock:

'and the rain descended, the floods came,
and the winds blew and beat on that house;
and it did not fall, for it was founded on the rock.'

But everyone who hears these sayings of Mine,
and does not do them, will be like a foolish man
who built his house on the sand:

'and the rain descended, the floods came,
and the winds blew and beat on that house;
and it fell.

And great was its fall.'

Matthew 7:24-27

"On Love,
I say to you who hear"

Love the LORD your God
with all your heart, with all your soul,
and..... with all your mind.

This is the first and great commandment.

And the second is like it:
You shall love your neighbor
as yourself.

On these two commandments
hang all the Law and the Prophets.

Matthew 22:37-40

But I tell you truly,

A new commandment I give to you,
that you love one another; as I have loved you,
that you also love one another.

By this all will know that you are My disciples,
if you have love for one another.

And

He who has My commandments and keeps
them, it is he who loves Me. And he who
loves me will be loved by My Father, and I will
love him and manifest Myself to him.

John 13:34-35 / John 14:21

Again I say to you

If you keep My commandments,
you will abide in My love, just as I have kept
My Father's commandments
and abide in His love.

And

This is My commandment,
that you love one another as I have loved you.

Greater love has no one than this,
than to lay down one's life for his friends.

And

You are My friends,
if you do whatever I command you.

John 15:10, 12-14

I say to you who hear:

Love your enemies,
do good to those who hate you,
bless those who curse you,
and pray for those who spitefully use you.

To him who strikes you on the one cheek,
offer the other also. And from him
who takes away your cloak,
do not withhold your tunic either.

Give to everyone who asks of you.
And from him who takes away your goods
do not ask them back.
And just as you want men to do to you,
you also do to them likewise.

Luke 6:27-31

If you love those who love you,
what credit is that to you?
For even sinners love those who love them.
and if you do good to those who do good to you,
what credit is that to you?
For even sinners do the same.

And if you lend to those from whom you hope
to receive back, what credit is that to you?
For even sinners lend to sinners
to receive as much back.

I say to you,
Love your enemies, do good,
and lend, hoping for nothing in return:
and your reward will be great,
and you will be sons of the Most High.

For He is kind to the unthankful and evil.
Therefore, be merciful,
just as your Father also is merciful.

Luke 6:32-36

You have heard that it was said,
You shall love your neighbor
and hate your enemy.

But I say to you, love your enemies,
bless those who curse you,
do good to those who hate you,
and pray for those who spitefully use you
and persecute you,

that you may be sons of your Father in heaven;
for He makes His sun rise on the evil
and on the good, and sends rain on the just
and on the unjust.

For if you love those who love you,
what reward have you?

Matthew 5:43-46a

On Light,
I say to you who hear,

I am the light of the world.

He who follows Me shall not walk in darkness,
but have the light of life.

Again, I Say to You

I have come as a light into the world,
that whoever believes in Me
should not abide in darkness.

And

While you have the light,
believe in the light,
that you may become
sons of light.

John 8:12 / John 12:46 / John 12:36

Now Learn This,

The lamp of the body is the eye.

Therefore, when your eye is good,
your whole body also is full of light.
But when your eye is bad,
your body also is full of darkness.

Therefore take heed
that the light which is in you
is not darkness.

If then your whole body
is full of light, having no part dark,

the whole body will be full of light,
as when the bright shining of a lamp
gives you light.

Luke 11:34, 36

Remember Always

You are the light of the world.
A city that is set on a hill
cannot be hidden.

Nor do they light a lamp
and put it under a basket,
but on a lampstand, and it gives light to all
who are in the house.

Therefore
Let your light so shine before men,
that they may see your good works
and glorify your Father in heaven.

Matthew 5:14-16

On Truth,
I say to you who hear,

No one, when he has lit a lamp,
covers it with a vessel or puts it under a bed,
but sets it on a lampstand,
that those who enter may see the light.

For nothing is secret that will not be revealed,
nor anything hidden that will not be known
and come to light.

Now learn this
Everyone practicing evil hates the light
and does not come to the light,
lest his deeds should be exposed.

But he who does the truth comes to the light,
that his deeds may be clearly seen,
that they have been done
in God.

Luke 8:16-17 / John 3:20-21

On Faith,
I say to you who hear,

Have faith in God.

For assuredly, I say to you, whoever says to this
mountain, "Be removed and be cast into the sea,"
and does not doubt in his heart, but believes
that those things he says will be done,
he will have whatever he says.

Remember Always

With men this is impossible,
but not with God; for with God
all things are possible.

Mark 11:22-23 / Matthew 19:26

Moreover

Consider the lilies, how they grow:
they neither toil nor spin; and yet I say to you,
even Solomon in all his glory
was not arrayed like one of these.

If then God so clothes the grass,
which today is in the field
and tomorrow is thrown into the oven,
how much more will He clothe you,
O you of little faith?

And do not seek what you should eat
or what you should drink,
nor have an anxious mind.

For all these things the nations of the world seek after,
and your Father knows that you need these things.

But seek the kingdom of God,
and all these things shall be added to you.

Do not fear, little flock, for it is your Father's
good pleasure to give you the kingdom.

Luke 12:27-32

On Believing,
I say to you who hear,

Whatever things you ask when you pray,
believe that you receive them,
and you will have them.

Again I say

Whatever things you ask in prayer,
believing, you will receive.

Now Listen Closely

If you can believe, all things are
possible to him who believes.

Mark 11:24 / Matthew 21:22 / Mark 9:23

On Asking,
I say to you who hear,

Ask, and it will be given to you;
seek, and you will find;
knock, and it will be opened to you.

For everyone who asks receives,
and he who seeks finds,
and to him who knocks it will be opened.

Most assuredly, I say to you,
whatever you ask the Father in
My name He will give you.

Until now you have asked nothing in My name.

But I tell you truly

Ask, and you will receive,
that your joy may be full.

Matthew 7:7-8 / John 16:23,-24

On Giving,
I say to you who hear,

Give,
and it will be given to you:

good measure, pressed down,
shaken together, and running over

will be put into your bosom.

And Remember Always

With the same measure
that you use,

it will be measured
back to you.

Luke 6:38

On Charity,
I say to you who hear,

Do not do your charitable deeds before men,
to be seen by them.
Otherwise you have no reward
from your Father in heaven.

Therefore, when you do a charitable deed,
do not sound a trumpet before you
as the hypocrites do in the synagogues
and in the streets,
that they may have glory from men.

Assuredly, I say to you, they have their reward.

But when you do a charitable deed,
do not let your left hand know
what your right hand is doing,
that your charitable deed may be in secret;

and your Father who sees in secret
will Himself reward you openly.

Matthew 6:1-4

On Forgivness,
I say to you who hear,

If your brother sins against you, rebuke him;
And if he repents, forgive him,

And if he sins against you seven times in a day,
and seven times in a day returns to you, saying,
'I repent,' you shall forgive him.

Assuredly I say to you

If you forgive men their trespasses,
your heavenly Father will also forgive you.

But if you do not forgive men
their trespasses,

neither will your Father
forgive your trespasses.

Luke 17:3-4 / Matthew 6:14-15

Again I say

whenever you stand praying,
if you have anything against anyone,

forgive him,

that your Father in heaven
may also forgive you
your trespasses.

Truly, I say

If you do not forgive
neither will your Father in heaven
forgive your trespasses.

Mark 11:25-26

67   *The Teachings of Jesus*

On Prayer,
I say to you who hear,

...when you pray,
you shall not be like the hypocrites.
For they love to pray standing in the synagogues
and on the corners of the streets,
that they may be seen by men.

Assuredly, I say to you, they have their reward.

But you, when you pray, go into your room,
and when you have shut your door,
pray to your Father who is in the secret place;
and your Father who sees in secret
will reward you openly.

And when you pray, do not use
vain repetitions as the heathen do.
For they think that they will be heard
for their many words.

Therefore do not be like them.
For your Father knows
the things you have need of
before you ask Him.

Matthew 6:5-8

Now Listen Closely

In this manner, therefore, pray:

Our Father in heaven, Hallowed be Your name.

Your kingdom come. Your will be done.
On earth as it is in heaven.

Give us this day our daily bread.

And forgive us our debts,
As we forgive our debtors.

And do not lead us into temptation,
But deliver us from the evil one.

For Yours is the kingdom and the power
and the glory forever.

Amen.

Matthew 6:9-13

On Fasting,
I say to you who hear,

do not be like the hypocrites,
with a sad countenance.

For they disfigure their faces
that they may appear to men to be fasting.

Assuredly, I say to you, they have their reward.

But you, when you fast,

anoint your head and wash your face,
so that you do not appear to men to be fasting,
but to your Father who is in the secret place;

and your Father who sees in secret
will reward you openly.

Matthew 6:16-18

On Loyalty,
I say to you who hear,

No one can serve two masters;
for either he will hate the one
and love the other,

or else he will be loyal to the one
and despise the other.

You cannot serve God and man.

Now Learn This

Every kingdom divided against itself
is brought to desolation,

and every city or house
divided against itself will not stand.

Matthew 6:24 / Matthew 12:25

71

On Marriage,
I say to you who hear,

He who made them at the beginning
made them male and female,
and said,

For this reason
a man shall leave his father and mother
and be joined to his wife,
and the two shall become one flesh..

So then, they are no longer two
but one flesh.

Therefore
what God has joined together,
let not man separate.

Matthew 19:4-6

On Children,
I say to you who hear,

Whoever receives one little child
in My name receives Me.

And

Whoever causes one of these little ones
who believe in Me to sin, it would be better
for him if a millstone were hung around his neck,
and he were drowned in the depth of the sea.

Therefore

Take heed that you do not despise
one of these little ones, for I say to
you that in heaven their angels
always see the face of My Father
who is in heaven.

Matthew 18:5,6,10

On Divorce,
I say to you who hear,

Moses,
because of the hardness of your hearts,
permitted you to divorce your wives,

but from the beginning
it was not so.

And I say to you,
whoever divorces his wife,
except for sexual immorality,
and marries another, commits adultery;
and whoever marries her
who is divorced commits adultery.

Matthew 19:8b-9

On Adultery,
I say to you who hear,

You have heard
that it was said to those of old,

'You shall not commit adultery.'

But I say to you,

that whoever looks at a woman
to lust for her

has already committed adultery
with her in his heart.

Matthew 5:27-28

75

On Worry,
I say to you who hear,

do not worry about your life,
what you will eat or what you will drink;
nor about your body, what you will put on.

Is not life more than food and the
body more than clothing?

Which of you by worrying
can add one cubit to his stature?

Consider the lilies of the field,
how they grow: they neither toil nor spin;
and yet I say to you that even Solomon
in all his glory was not arrayed like one of these.
Now if God so clothes the grass of the field,
which today is, and tomorrow is
thrown into the oven,
will He not much more clothe you,

O you of little faith?

Matthew 6:25, 27, 28-30

Therefore I say again

do not worry, saying,

"What shall we eat?' or "What shall we drink?'
or "What shall we wear?'

For your heavenly Father knows
that you need all these things.

Seek first the kingdom of God
and His righteousness, and
all these things shall be added to you.

Therefore do not worry about tomorrow,
for tomorrow will worry about its own things.
Sufficient for the day
is its own trouble.

Matthew 6:31-34

On Anger,
I say to you who hear,

You have heard
that it was said to those of old,
You shall not murder, and whoever murders
will be in danger of the judgment.

But I say to you
that whoever is angry with his brother
without a cause shall be in danger
of the judgment.

Therefore if you bring your gift to the altar,
and there remember that your brother
has something against you,
leave your gift there before the altar,
and go your way.

First be reconciled to your brother,
and then come and offer your gift.

Matthew 5:21-22a, 23-24

On Revenge,
I say to you who hear,

You have heard that it was said,

An eye for an eye and
a tooth for a tooth.

But I tell you not to resist an evil person.

But whoever slaps you on your right cheek,
turn the other to him also.

If anyone wants to sue you
and take away your tunic,
let him have your cloak also.

And whoever compels you to go one mile,
go with him two.

Give to him who asks you,
and from him who wants to borrow from you
do not turn away.

Matthew 5:38-42

On Swearing,
I say to you who hear,

Again you have heard
that it was said to those of old,

"You shall not swear falsely, but shall
perform your oaths to the Lord.'

But I say to you, do not swear at all:
neither by heaven, for it is God's throne;
nor by the earth, for it is His footstool;
or by Jerusalem, for it is the city of the great King.

Nor shall you swear by your head,
because you cannot make one hair white or black.

But let your "Yes' be Yes,' and your "No," "No.'

For whatever is more than these is from the evil one.

Matthew 5:33-37

On Judgment,
I say to you who hear,

Judge not,
and you shall not be judged.

Condemn not,
and you shall not be condemned.

Forgive,
and you will be forgiven.

And If You Judge,

Do not judge according to appearance,
but judge with righteous judgment.

For with what judgment you judge,
you will be judged;

and with the measure you use,
it will be measured back to you.

Luke 6:37 / John 7:24 / Matthew 7:2

On Brotherhood,
I say to you who hear,

Why do you look at the speck in your
brother's eye, but do not perceive
the plank in your own eye?

Or how can you say to your brother,

"Brother, let me remove the speck
that is in your eye,"
when you yourself do not see the plank
that is in your own eye?

First remove the plank from your own eye,
and then you will see clearly
to remove the speck
that is in your brother's eye.

Luke 6:41-42

Moreover
if your brother sins against you,

go and tell him his fault
between you and him alone.

If he hears you,
you have gained your brother.

But if he will not hear,
take with you one or two more,

that 'by the mouth of two or three witnesses
every word may be established.'

And if he refuses to hear them,
tell it to the church.

But if he refuses even to hear the church,
let him be to you like a heathen.

Matthew 18:15-17

Hear me, everyone and understand

A certain man went down
from Jerusalem to Jericho,
and fell among thieves,
who stripped him of his clothing,
wounded him, and departed,
leaving him half dead.

Now by chance
a certain priest came down that road.

And when he saw him,
he passed by on the other side.

Likewise a Levite,
when he arrived at the place,
came and looked, and passed by
on the other side.

But a certain Samaritan,
as he journeyed, came where he was.
And when he saw him,
he had compassion.

Luke 10:30-33

84

So he went to him and bandaged his wounds,
pouring on oil and wine;
and he set him on his own animal,
brought him to an inn, and took care of him.

On the next day, when he departed,
he took out two denarii,
gave them to the innkeeper, and said to him,

"Take care of him; and whatever more
you spend, when I come again,
I will repay you."

So, which of these three
do you think was neighbor
to him who fell among the thieves?

The man said, "He who showed mercy on him."
Then Jesus said to him, "Go and do likewise."

Be merciful, just as your Father also is merciful.

Luke 10:34-37 / Luke 6:36

On Discipleship,
I say to you who hear,

A disciple is not above his teacher,
but everyone who is perfectly trained
will be like his teacher.

"If anyone comes to Me
and does not hate his father and mother,
wife and children, brothers and sisters,
yes, and his own life also,
he cannot be My disciple.

And whoever does not bear his cross
and come after Me cannot be My disciple.
For which of you, intending to build a tower,
does not sit down first and count the cost,
whether he has enough to finish it--
lest, after he has laid the foundation,
and is not able to finish,
all who see it begin to mock him, saying,
"This man began to build and was not able to finish.'

So likewise, whoever of you does not forsake
all that he has cannot be My disciple.

Luke 6:40 / Luke 14:26-30, 33

Again,
I say to you who hear,

Whoever desires to come after Me,
let him deny himself, and take up his cross,
and follow Me.

For whoever desires to save his life
will lose it, but whoever loses his life
for My sake and the gospel's will save it.

For what will it profit a man if he gains the
whole world, and loses his own soul?
Or what will a man give in exchange for his soul?

For whoever is ashamed of Me and My words
in this adulterous and sinful generation,
of him the Son of Man also will be ashamed
when He comes in the glory of His Father
with the holy angels.

Mark 8:34-38

On your Treasure in Heaven,
I say to you who hear

"Take heed and beware of covetousness,
for one's life does not consist in the
abundance of the things he possesses."

The ground of a certain rich man yielded plentifully.
And he thought within himself, saying,

"What shall I do, since I have no room
to store my crops?'

So he said, "I will do this: I will pull down my barns
and build greater, and there I will store
all my crops and my goods.
And I will say to my soul,
"Soul, you have many goods laid up for many years;
take your ease; eat, drink, and be merry."'
But God said to him,
"Fool! This night your soul will be required of you;
then whose will those things be
which you have provided?'

"So is he who lays up treasure for himself,
and is not rich toward God.

Luke 12:15b, 16b-21

88

Now Listen Closely

Do not fear, little flock,
for it is your Father's good pleasure
to give you the kingdom.

Sell what you have and give alms;
provide yourselves money bags
which do not grow old,

a treasure in the heavens
that does not fail, where no thief approaches
nor moth destroys. For where your treasure is,
there your heart will be also.

I Say Again

Do not lay up for yourselves treasures on
earth, where moth and rust destroy
and where thieves break in and steal;
but lay up for yourselves treasures in heaven,
where neither moth nor rust destroys
and where thieves do not break in and steal.
For where your treasure is,
there your heart will be also.

Luke 12:32-34 / Matthew 6:19-21

On Greatness,
I say to you who hear,

Whoever desires to become great
among you, let him be your servant.

And whoever desires to be first
among you, let him be your slave.

Just as the Son of Man, did not come to be
served, but to serve, and to give His life
a ransom for many.

Again I Say

He who is greatest among you
shall be your servant.

And whoever exalts himself
will be humbled, and he who humbles
himself will be exalted.

Matthew 20:26-28 / Matthew 23:11-12

My friends, Listen Closely

You call Me Teacher and Lord and you say well
for so I am. For I have given you an example,
that you should do as I have done to you.

Most assuredly, I say to you,
a servant is not greater than his master,
nor is he who is sent greater than he who sent him.

If you know these things,
blessed are you if you do them.

And Remember Always

Where two or three are gathered together
in My name, I am there in the midst of them.

John 13:13,15-17 / Matthew 18:20

Peace be with you

Then Jesus started walking and they followed Him

End of Message

MESSAGE V
The Kingdom of Heaven

*It is now mid afternoon, and as the waves begin to crash
against the shore Jesus turned around, and said...*

Now I want to tell you about
the Kingdom of Heaven.

Strive to enter through the narrow gate,
for many, I say to you, will seek to enter
and will not be able.

Luke 13:24

Listen Closely

Not everyone who says to Me,
'Lord, Lord,'
shall enter the kingdom of heaven,
but he who does the will of My Father in heaven.

Many will say to Me in that day, "Lord, Lord,
have we not prophesied in Your name,
cast out demons in Your name,
and done many wonders in Your name?

And then I will declare to them,
'I never knew you; depart from Me,
you who practice lawlessness!"

Matthew 7:21-23

Now Learn This

I desire mercy and not sacrifice.
For I did not come to call the righteous,
but sinners, to repentance...

What man of you, having a hundred sheep,
if he loses one of them,
does not leave the ninety-nine in the wilderness,
and go after the one which is lost until he finds it?

And when he has found it,
he lays it on his shoulders, rejoicing.
And when he comes home,
he calls together his friends and neighbors,
saying to them,

Rejoice with me,
for I have found my sheep which was lost!

I say to you that likewise there will be
more joy in heaven over one sinner who repents
than over ninety-nine just persons
who need no repentance.

Matthew 9:13 / Luke 15:4-7

The Kingdom of Heaven

Most assuredly, I say to you

unless one is born again,
he cannot see the kingdom of God.

Unless one is born of water and the Spirit,
he cannot enter the kingdom of God.

That which is born of the flesh is flesh, and
that which is born of the Spirit is spirit.

Assuredly, I say to you,
unless you are converted
and become as little children,

you will by no means
enter the kingdom of heaven.

Therefore whoever humbles himself
as this little child is the greatest
in the kingdom of heaven.

John 3:3, 5-6 / Matthew 18:3-4

96

Again I say to you,
whoever does not receive the kingdom of God
as a little child will by no means enter it.

How hard it is for those who have riches
to enter the kingdom of God!
For it is easier for a camel
to go through the eye of a needle
than for a rich man to enter the kingdom of God.

But take heed

The things which are impossible with
men are possible with God.

Luke 18:17, 24-25, 27

The Kingdom of Heaven

On Heaven,
I say to you who hear

The kingdom of heaven is like a certain king
who wanted to settle accounts with his servants.

When he had begun to settle accounts,
one was brought to him who owed him
ten thousand talents.

As he was not able to pay,
his master commanded that he be sold,
with his wife and children and all that he had,
and that payment be made.

The servant therefore fell down before him, saying,
'Master, have patience with me,
and I will pay you all.'

Then the master of that servant
was moved with compassion,
released him, and forgave him the debt.

Matthew 18:23-27

But that servant went out
and found one of his fellow servants
who owed him a hundred denarii;
and he laid hands on him
and took him by the throat, saying,

'Pay me what you owe!'

So his fellow servant fell down at his feet
and begged him, saying,

'Have patience with me, and I will pay you all.'

And he would not,
but went and threw him into prison
till he should pay the debt.

So when his fellow servants saw
what had been done, they were very grieved,
and came and told their master
all that had been done.

Matthew 18:28-31

The Kingdom of Heaven

Then his master,
after he had called him, said to him,

'You wicked servant!
I forgave you all that debt because you begged me.

Should you not also have had compassion
on your fellow servant, just as I had pity on you?'

And his master was angry,
and delivered him to the torturers
until he should pay all that was due to him.

So My heavenly Father also will do to you
if each of you, from his heart,
does not forgive his brother his trespasses.

Matthew 18:32-35

100

Again, the kingdom of heaven

is like a dragnet that was cast into the sea
and gathered some of every kind,
which, when it was full, they drew to shore;
and they sat down and gathered
the good into vessels, but threw the bad away.

So it will be at the end of the age.

The angels will come forth
to separate the wicked from the just.
And cast them into the furnace of fire.
There will be wailing and gnashing of teeth.

Matthew 13:47-50

The Kingdom of Heaven

Again, I Say

The kingdom of heaven is like a landowner

who went out early in the morning
to hire laborers for his vineyard.

Now when he had agreed with the laborers
for a denarius a day,
he sent them into his vineyard.

And he went out about the third hour
and saw others standing idle
in the marketplace, and said to them,

' You also go into the vineyard,
and whatever is right I will give you.'

So they went.

Matthew 20:1-4

Again he went out about the sixth
and the ninth hour, and did likewise.

And about the eleventh hour he went out
and found others standing idle,
and said to them,

'Why have you been standing here idle all day?'
They said to him, 'Because no one hired us.'
He said to them, 'You also go into the vineyard, and
whatever is right you will receive.'

So when evening had come,
the owner of the vineyard said to his steward,

'Call the laborers and give them their wages,
beginning with the last to the first.'

And when those came who were hired
about the eleventh hour,
they each received a denarius.

Matthew 20:5-9

The Kingdom of Heaven

But when the first came,
they supposed that they would receive more;
and they likewise received each a denarius.

And when they had received it,
they complained against the landowner, saying,

'These last men have worked only one hour,
and you made them equal to us who have
borne the burden and the heat of the day.'

But he answered one of them and said,

'Friend, I am doing you no wrong.
Did you not agree with me for a denarius?'
Take what is yours and go your way.
I wish to give to this last man
the same as to you.

Matthew 20:10-14

Remember Always,

the last will be first, and the first last.
For many are called but few chosen.

Matthew 20:16

The Kingdom of Heaven

Now, Listen Closely

The kingdom of heaven
shall be likened to ten virgins
who took their lamps and went out
to meet the bridegroom.

Now five of them were wise, and five were foolish.
Those who were foolish took their lamps
and took no oil with them,
but the wise took oil
in their vessels with their lamps.

But while the bridegroom was delayed,
they all slumbered and slept.
And at midnight a cry was heard:
Behold, the bridegroom is coming;
go out to meet him!
Then all those virgins arose and trimmed their
lamps. And the foolish said to the wise,
Give us some of your oil,
for our lamps are going out.

Matthew 25:1-8

But the wise answered, saying,
No, lest there should not be enough
for us and you;
but go rather to those who sell,
and buy for yourselves.

And while they went to buy,
the bridegroom came, and those who were ready
went in with him to the wedding;
and the door was shut.

Afterward the other virgins came also, saying,
Lord, Lord, open to us!
But he answered and said,
Assuredly, I say to you, I do not know you.

Watch therefore, for you know neither the day
nor the hour in which the Son of Man is coming.

Matthew 25:9-13

The Kingdom of Heaven

Again I say

The kingdom of heaven
is like a man who sowed good seed in his field;
but while men slept, his enemy came
and sowed tares among the wheat and went his way.

But when the grain had sprouted
and produced a crop,
then the tares also appeared.

So the servants of the owner came and said to him,
"Sir, did you not sow good seed in your field?
How then does it have tares?'
He said to them, 'An enemy has done this.'
The servants said to him,
"Do you want us then to go and gather them up?'

But he said,
"No, lest while you gather up the tares
you also uproot the wheat with them.
Let both grow together until the harvest,
and at the time of harvest I will say to the reapers,

"First gather together the tares and bind them
in bundles to burn them,
but gather the wheat into my barn.

Hear Me everyone and understand
He who sows the good seed is the Son of Man.

The field is the world,
the good seeds are the sons of the kingdom,
but the tares are the sons of the wicked one.

The enemy who sowed them is the devil,
the harvest is the end of the age,
and the reapers are the angels.
Therefore as the tares are gathered
and burned in the fire,
so it will be at the end of this age.

The Son of Man will send out His angels,
and they will gather out of His kingdom
all things that offend,
and those who practice lawlessness,
and will cast them into the furnace of fire.
There will be wailing and gnashing of teeth.

Then the righteous will shine forth as the sun
in the kingdom of their Father.
He who has ears to hear, let him hear!

Matthew 13:24-30, 37-43

The Kingdom of Heaven

Now let these Words sink down in your ears

Blessed are the poor in spirit,
For theirs is the kingdom of heaven.

Blessed are those who mourn,
For they shall be comforted.

Blessed are the meek,
For they shall inherit the earth.

Blessed are those who hunger
and thirst for righteousness,
For they shall be filled.

Blessed are the merciful,
For they shall obtain mercy.

Matthew 5:3-7

Blessed are the pure in heart,
For they shall see God.

Blessed are the peacemakers,
For they shall be called sons of God.

Blessed are those who are persecuted
for righteousness' sake,
For theirs is the kingdom of heaven.

Blessed are you when they revile and persecute you,
and say all kinds of evil against you falsely
for My sake.

Rejoice and be exceedingly glad,
for great is your reward in heaven.

Matthew 5:8-12a

My Friends Listen Closely

Let not your heart be troubled;
you believe in God, believe also in Me.
In My Father's house are many mansions;
if it were not so, I would have told you.

I go to prepare a place for you.
And if I go and prepare a place for you,
I will come again and receive you to Myself;
that where I am, there you may be also.

And where I go you know,
and the way you know.

John 14:1-4

Remember Always

I AM the Way, the Truth and the Life
No one comes to the Father, except through Me.

John 14:6

Peace be with you

Then Jesus started walking and they followed Him

End of Message

MESSAGE VI

The End Times

While the sun was setting over the water,
the sounds of the late afternoon waves
created a calmness over the crowd of Believers.
As the birds were circling overhead
Jesus turned around, and said...

Now I want to tell you about the End Times

I am the Alpha and the Omega,
the Beginning and the End,
the First and the Last.

Revelation 1:8, 11

I Say to You Truly,

Take heed and beware that no one deceives you.
For many will come in My name, saying,
'I am the Christ' and will deceive many.

And you will hear of wars and rumors of wars.
See that you are not troubled;
for all these things must come to pass,
but the end is not yet.

For nation will rise against nation,
and kingdom against kingdom.
And there will be famines, pestilences,
and earthquakes in various places.
All these are the beginning of sorrows.

And then many will be offended,
will betray one another and will hate one another.
Then many false prophets will rise up
and deceive many
And because lawlessness will abound,
the love of many will grow cold.

But he who endures to the end shall be saved.

Matthew 24:4-13

Again I Say

If anyone says to you,
Look, here is the Christ! or There!
do not believe it.

For false christs and false prophets will rise
and show great signs and wonders
to deceive, if possible, even the elect.

See, I have told you beforehand.

Therefore if they say to you,
Look, He is in the desert! do not go out; or
Look, He is in the inner rooms! do not believe it.

For as the lightning comes from the east
and flashes to the west, so also
will the coming of the Son of Man be.

Matthew 24: 23-27

The End Times

Now Listen Closely

...when you hear of wars and commotions,
do not be terrified; for these things
must come to pass first,
but the end will not come immediately."

...nation will rise against nation,
and kingdom against kingdom.

And there will be great earthquakes
in various places, and famines and pestilences;
and there will be fearful sights
and great signs from heaven.

Luke 21:9-11

But before all these things,
they will lay their hands on you
and persecute you, delivering you up
to the synagogues and prisons.

You will be brought before kings and rulers
for My name's sake.
But it will turn out for you
as an occasion for testimony.

Therefore settle it in your hearts not to meditate
beforehand on what you will answer;
for I will give you a mouth and wisdom
which all your adversaries will not be able
to contradict or resist.

Luke 21:12-15

The End Times

"I Tell You the Truth,"

You will be betrayed even by parents and
brothers, relatives and friends; and they will
put some of you to death.

And you will be hated by all for My name's sake.
But not a hair of your head shall be lost.

By your patience possess your souls.

But when you see Jerusalem surrounded by
armies, then know that its desolation is near.

Then let those who are in Judea flee to the mountains,
let those who are in the midst of her depart, and
let not those who are in the country enter her.

For these are the days of vengeance,
that all things which are written may be fulfilled.

Luke 21:16-22

And there will be signs in the sun, in the moon,
and in the stars; and on the earth distress of nations,
with perplexity, the sea and the waves roaring;
men's hearts failing them from fear
and the expectation of those things
which are coming on the earth,
for the powers of the heavens will be shaken.

And

Then they will see the Son of Man
coming in a cloud with power and great glory.

Now when these things begin to happen,
look up and lift up your heads,
because your redemption draws near."

Luke 21:25-28

The End Times

"Now learn this parable from the fig tree: When its branch has already become tender and puts forth leaves, you know that summer is near.

So you also, when you see these things happening, know that it is near - at the doors!

Assuredly, I say to you, this generation will by no means pass away till all things take place.

Heaven and earth will pass away, but My words will by no means pass away. "But of that day and hour no one knows, not even the angels of heaven, but My Father only.

Matthew 24:32-36

*Watch therefore, for you do not know
what hour your Lord is coming.*

*But know this, that if the master of the house had
known what hour the thief would come,
he would have watched
and not allowed his house to be broken into.*

*Therefore you also be ready, for the Son of
Man is coming at an hour you do not expect.*

Now, Listen Closely

*These things I have spoken to you,
that in Me you may have peace.
In the world you will have tribulation;
but be of good cheer,
For, I have overcome the world.*

Matthew 24:42-44 / John 16:33

Peace be with you

Then Jesus knelt down to pray

End of Message

MESSAGE VII
The Holy Spirit

*The day is now ending and as the Moon begins
to rise over the water, a calm peace
could be felt everywhere and among everyone, and then...*

Jesus stood up, and said...

Now I want to tell you about the Holy Spirit

The Helper, the Holy Spirit,
whom the Father will send in My name,
He will teach you all things,
and bring to your remembrance
all things that I said to you.

John 14:26

Now Learn This

Every sin and blasphemy will be forgiven men,
but the blasphemy against the Spirit
will not be forgiven men.

Anyone who speaks a word
against the Son of Man, it will be forgiven him;
but whoever speaks against the Holy Spirit,
it will not be forgiven him, either in this age,
or in the age to come.

"Assuredly, I say to you, all sins will be forgiven
the sons of men,
and whatever blasphemies they may utter;
but he who blasphemes against
the Holy Spirit never has
forgiveness, but is subject to eternal condemnation"

Matthew 12:31-32 / Mark 3:28-29

Listen Closely

If you love Me, keep my commandments.
And I will pray to the Father,
and He will give you another Helper,
that He may abide with you forever.
so he who feeds on Me will live because of Me.

The Spirit of truth, whom the world cannot receive,
because it neither sees Him nor knows Him;
but you know Him, for He dwells
with you and will be in you.

And When they bring you
to the synagogues and magistrates and authorities,
do not worry about how or what you should answer,
or what you should say.

For the Holy Spirit will teach you
in that very hour what you ought to say.

John 14:15-17 / Luke 12:11-12

The Holy Spirit

My Friends

"I tell you the truth."
It is to your advantage that I go away;
for if I do not go away, the Helper will not come
to you; but if I depart, I will send Him to you.

And when He has come,
He will convict the world of sin,
and of righteousness, and of judgment:
of sin, because they do not believe in Me;
of righteousness, because I go to My Father
and you see Me no more; of judgment,
because the ruler of this world is judged.

When the Helper comes, to you from the Father,
The Spirit of truth who proceeds from the Father,
He will testify of Me.

John 16:7-11 / John 15:26

Assuredly, I say to you

When He,
the Spirit of truth, has come,
He will guide you into all truth;

for He will not speak on His own authority,
but whatever He hears He will speak;
and He will tell you things to come.

He will glorify Me,
for He will take of what is Mine
and declare it to you.

All things that the Father has are Mine.
Therefore I said that He will take of Mine
and declare it to you.

John 16:13-15

The Holy Spirit

My Friends, Remember Always

You did not choose Me, but I chose you
and appointed you that you should go
and bear fruit, and that your fruit should remain,
that whatever you ask the Father in My name
He may give you.

Peace I leave with you, My peace I give to you;
not as the world gives do I give to you.

Therefore
Let not your heart be troubled,
You believe in God, believe also in Me.

John 15:16 / John 14:1

Listen Closely

All authority has been given to me
in heaven and on earth.
Go therefore and make disciples of all nations,
baptizing them in the name of
the Father and of the Son and of the Holy Spirit,
teaching them to observe all things
that I have commanded you; and lo, I am with
you always, even to the end of the age.

Now, I Say to You Who Hear

Receive the Holy Spirit.

Matthew 28:18-20 / John 20:22

Peace be with you
forever and always

Then Jesus looked up to heaven
and said His last prayer

End of the Walk

The Holy Spirit

This Last Prayer from Jesus was for
His disciples and everyone else
who believes in His Word.

Jesus didn't pray for the world,
He prayed for those who follow Him.

Today, we call them,
The Believers

His
Last Prayer

John 17:1-26

Jesus prays for us all

Jesus lifted up His eyes to heaven and said

Father, the hour has come.
Glorify Your Son,

that Your Son also may glorify You,
as You have given Him authority
over all flesh, that He should give eternal life
to as many as You have given Him.

And this is eternal life, that they may know You,
the only true God, and Jesus Christ
whom You have sent.

I have glorified You on the earth.
I have finished the work which
You have given Me to do.

And now, O Father, glorify Me together with Yourself,
with the glory which I had with
You before the world was.

I have manifested Your name to the men
whom You have given Me out of the world.
They were Yours, You gave them to Me,
and they have kept Your word.

Now they have known that all things which
You have given Me are from You.

For I have given to them the words which
You have given Me; and they have received them,
and have known surely that I came forth from You;
and they have believed that You sent Me.

I pray for them.
I do not pray for the world
but for those whom You have given Me,
for they are Yours.

And all Mine are Yours, and Yours are Mine,
and I am glorified in them.

Now I am no longer in the world,
but these are in the world, and I come to You.

Holy Father, keep through Your name
those whom You have given Me,
that they may be one as We are.

Jesus prays for us all

I have given them Your word;
and the world has hated them
because they are not of the world,
just as I am not of the world.

I do not pray that You should take them out
of the world, but that You should keep them
from the evil one.

They are not of the world, just as
I am not of the world.

Sanctify them by Your truth. Your word is truth.

As You sent Me into the world,
I also have sent them into the world.
And for their sakes I sanctify Myself,
that they also may be sanctified by the truth.

I do not pray for these alone,
but also for those who will believe in Me
through their word; that they all may be one,

as You, Father, are in Me, and I in You;
that they also may be one in Us,
that the world may believe that You sent Me.

And the glory which You gave Me
I have given them,
that they may be one just as We are one:

I in them, and You in Me;
that they may be made perfect in one,

and that the world may know that You
have sent Me, and have loved them as
You have loved Me.

Jesus prays for us all

Father,
I desire that they also whom You gave Me
may be with Me where I am, that they may behold
My glory which You have given Me;

for You loved Me
before the foundation of the world.

O righteous Father!
The world has not known You,
but I have known You;
and these have known that You sent Me.

And I have declared to them Your name,
and will declare it,
that the love with which You loved Me
may be in them, and
I in them."

Amen

After the Lord had spoken with them,
He was received up into heaven,
and sat down at the right hand of God.

-Mark 16:19

There are also many other things that Jesus did,
which if they were written one by one,
I suppose that even the world itself
could not contain the books
that would be written.

John 21:25

The mighty words and works of Jesus Christ

When John the Baptist had heard in prison
about the works of Christ,
he sent two of his disciples
and said to Him,
"Are You the Coming One,
or do we look for another?"

Jesus answered and said to them,

Go and tell John the things which you hear and see:

The blind see and the lame walk;
the lepers are cleansed and the deaf hear;
the dead are raised up
and the poor have the gospel preached to them.

And blessed is he
who is not offended because of Me.

Matthew 11:2-6

"Who do men say that I, the Son of Man, am?"

*So they said, "Some say John the Baptist,
some Elijah, and others Jeremiah or
one of the prophets."*

*He said to them,
"But who do you say that I am?"*

*Simon Peter answered and said,
"You are The Christ,
the Son of the living God."*

*Blessed are you Simon Bar Jonah,
for flesh and blood
has not revealed this to you,*

*but My Father
who is in heaven.*

Matthew 16:13-17

When Jesus departed from there,
two blind men followed Him,
crying out and saying,
Son of David,
have mercy on us!"

And when He had come into the house,
the blind men came to Him.

And Jesus said to them,
"Do you believe that I am able to do this?"
They said to Him, "Yes, Lord."

Then He touched their eyes, saying,
"According to your faith let it be to you."

And their eyes were opened.

Matthew 9:27-29

Now when Jesus had entered Capernaum,
a centurion came to Him, pleading with
Him, saying, "Lord, my servant is lying at
home paralyzed, dreadfully tormented."

And Jesus said to him, "I will come and heal him."

The centurion answered and said,
"Lord, I am not worthy that You
should come under my roof.
But only speak a word, and my
servant will be healed.
For I also am a man under authority, having
soldiers under me. And I say to this one,
"Go,' and he goes; and to another, "Come,' and he
comes; and to my servant, "Do this,' and he does it."

When Jesus heard it, He marveled,
and said to those who followed,
"Assuredly, I say to you, I have not found
such great faith, not even in Israel!
Then Jesus said to the centurion,
"Go your way; and as you have
believed, so let it be done for you."
And his servant was healed that same hour.

Matthew 8:5-10,13

145

While He was still speaking,
someone came from the ruler of the
synagogue's house, saying to him,
"Your daughter is dead. Do not trouble the Teacher."

But when Jesus heard it, He answered him, saying,
"Do not be afraid; only believe, and she will be made well."

When He came into the house,
He permitted no one to go in
except Peter, James, and John,
and the father and mother of the girl.

Now all wept and mourned for her; but He said,
"Do not weep; she is not dead, but sleeping."
And they ridiculed Him, knowing that she was dead.
But He put them all outside, took her
by the hand and called, saying,
"Little girl, arise."

Then her spirit returned, and she arose immediately.

Luke 8:49-55

Now it happened on the next day,
when they had come down from the mountain,
that a great multitude met Him.

Suddenly a man from the multitude cried out, saying,
"Teacher, I implore You,
look on my son, for he is my only child.
And behold, a spirit seizes him, and he suddenly
cries out; it convulses him so that he foams
at the mouth; and it departs from him
with great difficulty, bruising him.

So I implored Your disciples to cast it out,
but they could not."

Then Jesus answered and said,
"O faithless and perverse generation,
how long shall I be with you and bear with you?
Bring your son here."

And as he was still coming, the demon
threw him down and convulsed him.
Then Jesus rebuked the unclean spirit, healed
the child, and gave him back to his father.

Luke 9:37-42

147

Jesus departed...
...and went up on the mountain and sat down there.

Then great multitudes came to Him,
having with them the lame, blind,
mute, maimed, and many others;
and they laid them down at Jesus' feet,
and He healed them.

So the multitude marveled when they saw the mute
speaking, the maimed made whole, the lame walking,
and the blind seeing; and they glorified God.

Matthew 15:29-31

When it was evening,
His disciples came to Him, saying,
"This is a deserted place, and the hour is already late.
Send the multitudes away,
that they may go into the villages
and buy themselves food."

But Jesus said to them,
"They do not need to go away.
You give them something to eat."

And they said to Him, "We have here
only five loaves and two fish."
He said, "Bring them here to Me."

Then He commanded the multitudes to sit down
on the grass. And He took the five loaves and the
two fish, and looking up to heaven, He blessed
and broke and gave the loaves to the disciples;
and the disciples gave to the multitudes.
So they all ate and were filled, and they took
up twelve baskets full of the fragments that
remained. Now those who had eaten were about
five thousand men, besides women and children.

Matthew 14:15-21

Conclusions in Christ

Eventually, we will all come to conclusions about our life.
We already know in the end . . . we won't get out of here alive.
However, we don't know, for sure -- in the beginning what our
life is really about, or where we might end up.

We now know the beginning of our life is directly shaped by
our parents, our teachers, our friends as well as society.

One child is raised in the church and then, as an adult, they do
violent things to our society, and end up in prison. Yet another
child is raised *outside* of the church, and after discovering
the message of Jesus, they go on to become an instrument of
healing, bringing glory and honor to the Kingdom of God.

As Christians, I believe we must "conclude for ourselves"
what we believe to be true, and then be the *living example* of
that *divine truth.* Jesus said, "You are the light of the world, "
for others to see, especially our family, friends and those who
are lost. Remember, people take our example more seriously
than our advice.

I have read several hundred books on the subject of *Personal
Excellence* and *Success in Life,* and I have found nothing that
compares to the *profound truth* so *plainly taught* by Jesus as
outlined in the Red Letters of the New King James Bible.

In all of recorded history, no *one man* has impacted the hearts of men and women as Jesus has. Nor has anyone else ever been declared the Son of God -- through the *life they lived,* and the *lessons they taught* -- as Jesus has.

So, I conclude, and I declare that I am a Christian, and my life in Christ has been tested and proven to me, to be true. I find every word Jesus said to be believable and applicable in my daily life; and I will continue to be the best example I can, in Christ Jesus.

If you consider yourself a Christian, I ask you to join me and let us *become the example* for the world to see. When we do this, *our Father in Heaven* is glorified, and we will all come together as *One Flock,* with *One Shepherd.*

May God Bless you in all that you do...

I am, Your Brother in Christ,

    -Rev. Terry Allan Christian

Remember what Jesus said . . .

"The hour is coming, and now is,
when the true worshipers will worship
the Father in spirit and truth
for the Father is seeking such to worship Him."

-About the Composer-
Rev. Terry Allan Christian

Terry developed a severe stuttering problem while growing up in a *violently dysfunctional* family. This led him to drop out of high school at 16 and leave home - with little hope of any success. His life changed forever when, at 23, he met Jesus in a *life-altering dream,* where he was given *the vision of teaching*, and *helping everyone he meets.* He was told that he would one day become a teacher of Christian Principles.

During the next 30 years, he constantly studied the Red Letter Edition of the King James Version Bible, always concentrating on the words of Jesus and the *example of His actions*.

Terry retired in September 2000, after spending twenty years traveling throughout America and Canada as a motivational speaker, teaching over 2500 personal and professional development seminars. Today, he teaches Christian-based workshops where only the **words of Jesus** are used.

Reverend Christian devotes his time to those seeking Christian Counseling and a deeper understanding of the Teachings of Jesus.

His mission is to H-E-L-P - Help Everyone Live Peacefully

He does this by "helping" families and congregations come together in love, as one body, in one accord, to perform a greater work for Christ! **For more information visit www.RevChristian.com.**

Special Thanks

In Love, Light & Truth, I thank. . .

• **My Mother,** (*now deceased*) for her *example* of Christ-like love. She was the one who brought me to church where I was saved, and she was the one who first showed me the Red Letters.

• **My daughter** Kerry, *for giving me the honor* of being her *earthly father.* I believe, *being her father* has made me a *better man*, and *as my Father in Heaven loves me... I love her.*

• **Benjamin Kittleson**, *for being my friend and brother in Christ; as well as for his steadfast patience* as we constantly edited and improved this book. *I thank God everyday for sending him to help .*

• **Annette Reid**, *for being my prayer partner and special friend* who strives to always find God's way in her dedication to serve in the Word. Her *light in life* is inspiring to watch. I thank God for her *constant prayers* for, and gifts to our ministry.

• **My Christian brothers,** Adam Guerrero, Mark Allbright and Don Clark for their help and friendship over the last 25 years.

• **The Body of Christ,** for those who have suddenly appeared in my life, to lift me and support me in the development of this ministry and to those who have not judged me, but rather, helped me, with my walk in Christ.

A Closing Message from
Rev. Terry Allan Christian

Truly, I want to thank you for taking the time to read this book! My mission in life is to travel wherever God sends me; freely teaching the lessons outlined in this book. Therefore, if you believe this book has positively touched your life, then I want to ask you for 3 things...

1.   **I ask for your prayers**, so our Heavenly Father will know we are in agreement together, and that we are helping the Body of Christ become *stronger and better*.

Jesus said,
"If two of you agree on earth concerning anything that they ask, it will be done for them by my Father in Heaven."

Matthew 18:19

2.   **I ask you to reach out** and *touch someone* that you *don't know* and show them the *Love, Light and Truth* of *Christ* by your example of a TRUE CHRISTIAN.

3.   **I ask you to assist** our ministry in this *mission* to H-E-L-P *Helping Everyone Live Peacefully...*

Remember what Jesus said,
"Give, and it will be given to you: good measure, pressed down, shaken together, and running over will be put into your bosom. With the same measure that you use, it will be measured back to you.

Luke 6:38

From the Heart

"Whatever things you ask when you pray;
believe that you will have them."
-Jesus Christ

To send us a Prayer from your Heart,
visit our website:

www.FoundationsforLife.org/prayers.html

To share a Gift from your Heart,
visit our website:

www.FoundationsforLife.org/gifts.html

156

A LOVING EXPERIENCE FOR THE WHOLE FAMILY!

Walking with the *Master*

This *Live Multi-Media* **Christian Workshop**

reveals the *Teachings of Jesus* in His own words...

Rev. Terry Allan Christian's foundation lesson in this message is one of *Love, Light and Truth*, the same *spiritual message* Jesus spoke of with His disciples in the Book of John. (c.v.-3:21 / 4:24 / 13:34-35)

Throughout this message, Reverend Christian guides you through the profound Teachings of Jesus and explains the *healing power* of *love and forgiveness* that changes our lives. He compels everyone who attends to *submit to one another* in love, light and truth as members of *one family*, in the Body of Christ... as an example for others to follow.

Bring your family and friends, and participate in a healing, loving experience that everyone will remember for the rest of their lives.

Program Length (varied by event): 30 mins. - 3 hours

The message, *Walking with the Master* also includes
Reverend Christian's *personal testimony* of his 46-day fast.
This is one testimony you don't want to miss . . .

To schedule him for your church event, send an email to:
Information@FoundationsForLife.org.

To schedule Reverend Christian
for your Church or Bible-Study group
visit
www.FoundationsForLife.org

To ask him questions,
visit
www.HelpinChrist.com

Now available in full color eBook & Audiobook formats,
visit
www.WDJS.info